AN OPENING IN THE VERTICAL WORLD

Also by Roger Greenwald

Poetry

Connecting Flight
Slow Mountain Train
The Half-Life

Poetry in Translation

The Silence Afterwards: Selected Poems of Rolf Jacobsen
Stone Fences, by Paal-Helge Haugen (trans. with William Mishler)
The Time in Malmö on the Earth, by Jacques Werup
Wintering with the Light, by Paal-Helge Haugen
Did I Know You? Thirty-one poems by Rolf Jacobsen
Through Naked Branches: Selected Poems of Tarjei Vesaas
North in the World: Selected Poems of Rolf Jacobsen
Picture World, by Niels Frank
Meditations on Georges de La Tour, by Paal-Helge Haugen
Guarding the Air: Selected Poems of Gunnar Harding
Through Naked Branches: Selected Poems of Tarjei Vesaas, Revised Edition

Fiction in Translation

A Story About Mr. Silberstein, by Erland Josephson
I Miss You, I Miss You! by Peter Pohl and Kinna Gieth (young-adult novel)

ROGER GREENWALD

An Opening
in the Vertical World

BLACK WIDOW PRESS
BOSTON

Poems and Notes copyright © 1993, 2004, 2006, 2015, 2021, 2022, 2024 by Roger Greenwald. Edition © 2024 by Black Widow Press. All rights reserved.

This book, or parts thereof, may not be reproduced in any form or by any means electronic, digital, or mechanical, including photocopy, scanning, recording, or any information storage and retrieval system, without written permission from the publisher except in the case of brief quotations embodied in critical articles and reviews. For information, contact Black Widow Press, 9 Spring Lane, Boston, MA 02109.

Black Widow Press is an imprint of Commonwealth Books, Inc., Boston, MA. Distributed to the trade by NBN (National Book Network) throughout North America, Canada, and the U.K. All Black Widow Press books are printed on acid-free paper, and glued into bindings. Black Widow Press and its logo are registered trademarks of Commonwealth Books, Inc.

Joseph S. Phillips and Susan J. Wood, Ph.D., Publishers
www.blackwidowpress.com

Cover image: Etching "Spring Sans Souci" © 1978 by Ed Bartram. Used by permission of the artist. Author photo: Alf Magne Heskja

Library of Congress Control Number: 2024942716
ISBN-13: 979-8-9911391-0-6

This book has been composed in Minion Pro.
The paper used in this publication meets the minimum requirements of ANSI / NISO Z39.48-1992 (R 1997) (Permanence of Paper).

Printed in the United States of America

10 9 8 7 6 5 4 3 2 1

for Dr. Bjørnar Hassel

Contents

In the Crowd   11

I   Layover

1969	15
Layover	16
Spring Flowers at Pompeii	18
The Dogs of Pompeii	19
Delicious Denmark	20
Stone, Life	21
Without	22
The Human Genome	23
Why I Am Not an Indian	24
Seeing Me	25

II   Blue Vehicle

Lens	31
Biology	32
Rollback	33
Office Workers Looking at the Sky	34
Blue Vehicle	35
Overcome	37
Extreme Measures	38
Welcome Back / Come Again	39
Bergen, Port and Portal	40
The Voice	41
The Shop for Forgotten Things	42
Twilight's Over	43
In the Parking Lot near the Cultural Center	44

...

III   Whisper Dance
Who Are the Poets?   *47*
    You Don't Have to Be Leonard Cohen   *48*
    Memento Amori   *49*
    Bananas   *50*
    Friday Night   *51*
    My Head   *52*
Wrong Directions   *53*
Side Trips   *54*
Past   *55*
Questions   *57*
Baul   *58*
Reunion   *59*
In the Small of the Night   *60*
Art Institute   *61*
That Time of the Night (CBC Radio)   *62*
Whisper Dance   *64*

Notes   *69*

Acknowledgments   *73*

AN OPENING IN THE VERTICAL WORLD

In the Crowd

Not to have one
    person's name to say.
To stand in the crowd before
    the doors are opened,
to hear their language as though
    you were saying their words
yourself, to smell their skin their
    hair the damp wool
sweaters: to smell the infants
    they were, see their parents
in their faces, moving hands, the weight
    shifting to the other hip, to feel
them pressing behind you
    gently as the doors are opened, they
do not push forward but
    do not avoid the bodies either,
you are carried with them
    into the large hall, into
the music, they go with their friends,
    with their children, with
you in their midst, you in
    your leather jacket and its many pockets,
you have room for kleenex and matches,
    you have your festival pass and room
for pens and lip balm and your book
    with five hundred addresses in the world,
the world outside, which is not
    here with you, the world
where some few people know your name
    though you have no one's name to say
as a man with a long mountain horn
    lifts it, lifts it, puts his lips
against it and the mountain

    sounds, you hear its song as though
you were calling its notes
    yourself, it does not avoid
your body, it presses gently
    against you, and a woman
steps forward to sing, at any moment
    she will call out, she will
call the beginning
    of something you belong to.

I
Layover

1969

As the red line pulled by the tiny airplane
arcs toward Montreal on the KLM monitor,
the towns of New York State appear to the south:
Plattsburgh, Ithaca, Woodstock, Bethel.
When you fly over them even their lights
seem to be outposts of another kind, American
attempts at company among the nocturnal lakes.
That farmer understood it would be a large conversation,
accompanied by music on the loneliest of continents.
But by now the tiny airplane has crossed Labrador,
pushed into the blue Atlantic; and the outside temperature
is minus fifty-nine.

Layover

Back to the crowd at Schipol, stretched out
on a bench, one arm through a loop
of my knapsack, one in the loophole
called dream. At eighteen
you can fling yourself down as you like,
like your clothes, you're a jacket
scarcely filled. Now I'm not supposed
to be in a state of travel, only traveling
from point O to point M, and I should catch
connecting flights without the waste
of layovers.

In the dream on the bench
I am falling asleep, I am only five
in the yellow room at the end of the hall.
Far away there's a rustling, I know now
that Grandpa must have been spreading out his paper,
but the sound then was magnified and patterned
in a way I almost grasped, voices through a wall,
threatening because they mounted, or because
I couldn't catch the words. He turned the pages—
reading right to left until the letters found their way
back to me. They said, "You must sleep now, sleep."

Did I dream then of the morning, my shoes
with their rounded noses on the newly asphalted path?—
the soft flannel lining of my brown wool cap
snug on my forehead so the curved brim shaded
perfect vision in clear air?

It wasn't my intention to wander. I just
got detoured on my journey left to right.
I was heading east and got caught in a loop.

But I can still see him sitting in an easy chair
next to the lamp whose stainless-steel shaft
held a smoked-glass bowl that poured light
upward onto the plaster ceiling. I'm pretty sure
he's waiting for something.

Spring Flowers at Pompeii

Spring is walking away from you.
Though her white flowers have just opened
she is walking away as she gathers them in her cornucopia
and has been walking away for at least
nineteen hundred and nineteen years.
She is neither barefoot nor sandaled, but wearing
linen slippers as thin as the shift
that has slipped off her right shoulder
as she stretched out her hand to pluck another sprig.
Her shift is yellow, her cast-off tunic bone,
her basket a terra-cotta color that matches her hair,
crowned by a wreath of yellow flowers.
Over her shoulder you can glimpse her eyebrow
but she is not looking over her shoulder,
she is walking away from you and attending
to the sprig between her thumb and index finger
which she will bring to grace someone's table—
someone she was walking toward
when the heavens fell.

The Dogs of Pompeii

Unlike dogs set loose in the parks of Western cities
or those that run in packs in the small towns of France,
the dogs of Pompeii, which live among the dead and the tourists,
show no hostility to humans, or friendliness,
or any other interest. They visit
each other in their piss-marked Latin quadrants,
lie outdoors on warm paving stones
or indoors on cool marble,
and chase off intruders, pets whose excursions
make them strays in the eyes of the strays
squatting in the houses of departed magistrates,
merchants, surgeons, priests, cult devotees, gods and goddesses.
Here they will pass their generations unmoved
by the fear, aggression, or fantasies of owners
until their carefree descendants are buried once again
by Vesuvius.

Delicious Denmark

From a thousand feet up I could see the sailboats
I would not be on. Papers were free
listing films I wouldn't go to, and tourist brochures
informed of concerts I might discover had been cancelled.
Four thousand three hundred twenty-two
suntanned blondes refrained from speaking to me,
in fact averted their eyes, and their feet
glided the walking-street on invisible rails
like models powered by friction engines.
I suffered no defects other than a wakeful mind
and a longing for more than one sort
of connection. Something
must have conveyed these silently,
red lights heeded by the experienced engineers.

Stone, Life

There's nothing moving here, and what moves
I mistake: my eye thinks pigeon
as a seated girl's silken slipper
moves on marbled floor of oboed atrium.
Pianist, waitress, attendant of my flights,
I have no business anywhere, no cash
is paid me, schedule imposed:
You spot this in a blink, it's life only
I'm trying to recover but the stone
won't move. What stone.

Without

Without
consuming alcohol or pills
I wake up trembling
at the prospect of another day of good health in the sun,
the people of Copenhagen streaming over me.
I'm a pebble, to see the trembling of a rock
they'd have to be Martian rovers,
equipped with alpha-proton spectrometers
and programmed to be curious. The eyes
don't have it.

The Human Genome

I was dressed typographically:
black white and red.
People in the subway tried to read me
but I was a language
they didn't know and didn't
want to. Even so
they had a feeling I was full of
trykkfeil.

Why I Am Not an Indian

I am not an Indian because
you've never met one or you wouldn't ask.
I am not an Indian because
I am a Jew and don't ask
what percentage, when I say Jew
I mean through and through
though few who are Orthodox would say so.
It's true no one knows
where we came from and my mother's mother
with a tan could have looked Mongolian,
could have come from people who millennia before
wandered eastward with their horses and eventually rode
into the cowboy films of my New York childhood
where she, escaped from the pogroms,
held a sugar cube between her teeth
to sweeten her lemony Russian tea.
But no, I am not an Indian.
So look again. Look in.

Seeing Me

They say it's hard to see yourself and that is true,
but often what they mean is it's hard to know
how others see you. And I have watched them looking—
or not looking—long enough to report results.
I grant from the outset, however,
that my observer's gaze is part of what people notice
and react to or judge or project onto,
so that here as in quantum mechanics the instrument
affects the phenomena,
but in the macro world this is not so important
and I am bound to look in any case, for this
is my nature.
                    Tourists sometimes imagine
I'm a pickpocket, especially if I happen
to slow or swerve on the promenade
shortly after passing them, perhaps because
an interesting woman or language is walking along.
This shows how little they know of pickpockets,
since I have my glasses in one hand and may well
be working a toothpick with the other. And they have
no fixed destinations themselves but have been warned
and would like the satisfaction of spotting a thief.
The real ones, whom I often spot, know of course
that I'm a tourist, they just don't expect the antennas
derived from growing up in New York.
Pickpockets and snatchers—the ones with small sharp knives—
aren't the only people with private business, and the others
often think I'm a cop or agent: a potentially dangerous perception
but there's nothing I can do except stroll on, I don't know
what they're up to, but then, it's how they see me
that's the subject here.
                          It's surprising how many harmless or innocent
people view me with suspicion or at least feel discomfort

when they realize I am looking and can see them,
though many of these same people will complain about
their friends' or spouses' obtuseness. The older married sisters
of beautiful young women, for example, have "conversations" with me
that search out my intentions (as quaint as that may sound),
afraid I'm just passing through and am not serious, yet
equally afraid I'm not and I am. Their sisters also
are of two minds, since the Exotic Traveler
is not to be trusted but can be exciting
to use for a while and throw away. They may dream too
of rescue from their narrow home towns—
with all the ambivalence attached to leaving—
and not be aware of their underlying wish or plan,
to be rescued first and then cast off the knight because
they had to depend on him.
                                       There's hardly a person who doesn't
think I'm too serious, too intellectual, too emotional, or too sexual,
depending on where their lowest thresholds lie.
My childhood teachers thought I was too quick with quips,
whereas now even some friends express surprise
at humor in my poems. Or openness. Or warmth.
Many who know me professionally confuse
high standards with an attitude dourly judgmental,
while those I have confided in are so cognizant of,
or perhaps so impatient with, my unrelenting sorrow
that they forget whatever other traits may be visible.
Men are apt to act aggressively toward me, for reasons
they should be made to account for themselves. I know
they fantasize that I have many women they want and
others they've never seen or met,
and the married ones pretend to envy my single life, though none
has ever accepted my offer to trade places.
My students see me as younger and stricter than I am,
which may be good. Almost no one guesses I'm a writer

except when I'm scribbling in a café like now, and then
they make me out a reviewer. Poets, of course, exist only
as a category of self-description, no one believes
a person could be a poet, though people know
in a theoretical way that a poet must be a person.
This and not their inability to hear a voice from the page is why
they must go to readings before buying books: to make sure
the poet really exists.
                 I can suffer
from similar doubts, though not about poets. For instance,
I had to stand to one side for ten minutes in the Pollio Gelateria in
    Sorrento
to convince myself that the beauty filling cones
was not only flesh and blood, but friendly, unaffected, quick to laugh.
When I approached she grew almost stern, I thought, unless
it was just concentration on English. I would give a lot to be able
to read minds in these cases. Women have told me
how they've seen me, of course, but they speak
for themselves and cannot generalize.
My point here hasn't been
that I'm not seen as I see myself,
for that's universal, and as I started by saying,
it's true it's hard to see yourself and
I'm no exception. What's striking is
how little the way people see me relies
on what's visible, aside from my looking.
What they hear is also rarely what I've said,
but I'll let that wait, since it's advisable
to deal with only one species
of disappointment at a time.

II

Blue Vehicle

Lens

What do the mild clouds have to do
with the tight-pored skin of single mothers
struggling uphill with children on bikes?
Why am I grateful and resentful
toward those on their own who manage some smiles?
Why can't I imagine the broadcast tower
traversing the drifting clouds—
the limits to mind-over-matter
asserting themselves even in a relative world.
Can the fingers of two hands ever make a frame
wide-angle enough so one of the Sunday hikers
will look into my airy lens
and say PLEEZ?
The gifts I would give are rolling around
on the flagstones with a hollow sound
like discarded plastic soda bottles
toppled by the breeze.

Biology

Did life begin in clay or a shallow pond
of akvavit? Which came first,
the chicken or its DNA?
Can a scale become a feather, or must
a feather have a feathery father?
Likewise, can a lung adapt
to eight-hour shifts in an Oslo bar?
And can biology be transcended there
or is our bar behavior
entirely determined? Including
our indirect questions
to a woman who buses tables
while she studies biology.
Surely that's all the Krebs cycle can be good for,
aside from survival, which is not
enough. No, this is not your exam.
This is harder, this keeps going
as long as you do, this can't be
studied for, and it's pass-fail.
Your mark, by the way, will be delayed in the mail.

Rollback

Across the aisle, in a red ring-binder,
the diagram might show the Old Norse cosmos:
heaven and hell surround
a nucleus of middling life, unless of course
this is a eukaryotic cell, supporting
fibers paler than ash. Than blond.
She turns the page, forked entities
give the answer: chromosomes.
The signals aren't working
in the stretch past Vikersund, we roll
at under 40 K "for reasons
of safety." The well-known boy
with one bronze arm out to the end
of his willow flute is too intent
to notice the black office-block
or even the round snowy lake, with its central
island of erect pines. His note
is just about to sound. Just about.
She coughs, wrinkles her nose as she marks
a passage written in her own large hand.
I'll just go back two cars to the café,
and while she becomes a doctor I'll buy
some apple juice to relieve her cold.
I'll just go back
two cars to the café,
to the round lake,
the signals,
her hand
turning the page.

Office Workers Looking at the Sky

It's lunchtime and incredibly enough
Oslo's office people are on the sidewalks
talking looking up hurting their eyes
squinting through garbage bags sunglasses film-strips cardboard goggles.
Yes a partial eclipse of the sun of the light of the usual routine of the Oslo
    darkness.
The women are raising their arms with their viewers
you can see their hands clearly
the wedding bands glint under the quarter-disk of star
they are married married married every last one
of Oslo's office workers
the women, that is, for the men are older balding divorced
these women's husbands work elsewhere for better pay
and have affairs with yet other
office workers, women not out here now
I don't know where they are
I've never figured it out
and that's not the only thing.

Blue Vehicle

The figures moving across the overpass
are not women, they are two blossoms
of a plant I can't identify
in the half-darkness, their motion
parallax as my trolley rolls
toward the start of the long climb,
their upper torsos cone-shaped
like the flowers of the horse-chestnut,
their slight leaning forward not because
of the wind, for there is none,
but merely a sign of the sun's relation
to the concrete cloverleaf where they grow,
result of an elementary tropism.

Their heads dip as they make their way
or rather slide back
toward the city, the whole overpass
recedes toward the city and soon
disappears behind the window seal,
now it's the twilit harbor that spreads out
beyond the drop, its islands
with their rows of sleeping pleasure craft;
and the driver does not call the stops,
this is an extra run, she's not obliged
to adjust her speed to printed times,
we spin past trees and houses, rock face,
crossings, sport fields, woods and hills,
our two halves rock and sway,
the round joining part
turning in this dim interior,

back and forth in different increments
like the dial of a combination lock.

But this blue vehicle will never come apart. I'll go out
through my chosen door, it's suddenly strange
they're all on one side—
symmetry's beyond my view, fulfilled
only by a matching car
on adjacent tracks, which may or may not appear
before I leave, almost close enough to touch.

Overcome

Overcome at the spice rack, leaning on the freezer
moving for old ladies who want the boxed fish.
Though she was pedaling and may have seen
the motion as I took them off,
I think she heard the little click as the temple
of my sunglasses folded against the frame.
Slight smiles
passed in that second as bike and pedestrian
continued on their paths. I smile
as if it doesn't matter whether we stop
and because it matters, my voice is paralyzed.

I manage to look like a normal human being for the next fifteen minutes
until I'm facing all the packets and bottles,
the periodic table of condiments, each name a separate weight
that measures what I do not have:
ground or whole, leaf or flower, conversations in the night.
Must stay on my feet, wouldn't know what to say
to the paramedics: "The water is wide, guys,
and getting wider,
and all I can see is a lake behind
a screen of trees." Not in their manual.

I would have said:
"I didn't take them off to see you better,
but so you could see me. Can you see me?"

Leaning on the freezer
I keep thinking that the little click
of the safety is the last thing you hear.

Extreme Measures

Run Over

"If I have to get run over I guess I'd like it to be by you" I thought as the bike grazed past me down the steep block straight arms strong hands dirty-blond hair flapping around shoulders and I watched it slow to cross the level road round bottom in white pants on the black seat shadow in the groove before it raced down Tantalus Hill so the head vanished below the asphalt edge as I saw one of many futures in which inevitably I would say aloud "But I'm not willing to get run over not even by you."

In Charge

My beautiful pregnant neighbor is letting him have it eight floors below at the bicycle rack her tall kindly guy who has to stand still on his bike while she holds her own with one hand on a hip and dresses him down for whatever transgression's alleged so he's straightened and chastened before they set off toward the east for their evening the words inaudible up here behind my glass but the message clear as it is to him beyond all particulars.

If

Jogging by river sucking lozenge for the sugar boost I pass the sunbathers drunks and prampushers dogwalkers junkies other joggers strolling couples many ducks until a woman appears a ways off with straightforward gait in neat khakis small backpack her hands have short nails without polish the capable hands of someone in health care stop jogging start coughing and gasping bent over she's here now I whisper Help me inhaled a pastille do the Heimlich I don't have to show her she does it I spit out the lozenge from under my tongue extreme measures are needed in Oslo if a life's to be saved.

Welcome Back / Come Again

"Before you arrived, the weather
was so fine. Too bad
you couldn't come earlier.
Where have you been—oh, I know,
in that ugly place where you slave away—
I meant why there and not here.
And now that you're leaving
it's clearing again. You just about
have time for one long walk
this sunny evening in the forests
surrounding the city. Did you notice
that sound as though a woman
were coming through the trees and her silver earrings
rang faintly against themselves?
It was a small bird that's impossible
to see and has therefore never been named.
And the mirrored pines are almost perfectly
still now, there's a slight ripple but
we may as well keep going, you could wait
a long time before the water yielded glass
and anyway by then it might be dark.
Listen to the parchment of those aspen leaves
tapping like meek castanets.
Now you know why the water
kept moving. Maybe you should settle
somewhere like this. Not in the forest, of course
but within reach. It's a shame
you couldn't stay longer, tomorrow
the great Russian pianist is giving a concert. Next time
you'll have to come sooner. Next time
you ought to bring less work, see more friends,
admire their children, go to the movies.
You can come to dinner, we'll invite
people you know."

Bergen, Port and Portal

> "straddling the fjord that funnels its wealth"
> —*National Geographic*

—You can see it's a question
of a maritime city, said the Frenchman
to his wife among the fishmongers.
Above them stood the wing of Mt. Fløien,
and then the highest hill with its signal mast.

It's true the boats have come and gone
for nine hundred years, and even now
deliver fish and tourists, cousins and commuters.
But you will not find the riches in the warehouse,
nor the harbor in the harbor.
Look up, for this is an opening
in the vertical world. Fine lines of rain
have drawn the evergreens upward,
mist sinks over the cliff-rim, and smoke
rises from brick chimneys topped by slate.
Water runs down the hillsides and you walk up,
at the summit cairns stretch higher and you can read
a column of white puffs above the horizon
against a ladder of shaded cloud.
Nothing is horizontal here, even the sea
curves downward with the planet and the mountain lakes
tilt toward you in an access of polar blue.

Wherever you are in the dusk you will know
that meteor-sparks have lit the wooden houses.
When the wind sweeps in new weather
and church bells drown the steamship whistles,
offer up a song to remember
you are in Bergen, port and portal
in the vertical world.

The Voice

Power lines trace your line of sight,
high tension at the vanishing point.
Climbing-spikes in the poles
belong to a special character set:
braille for the feet—up and down
this alphabet like scales,
a language that leads to the clouds.

Gnash of soles on fine gravel;
you are moving past the trees
and the trees past you,
everything's turning, as Dr. E.
explained, depends on your frame of view.

What does this have to do with your voice,
other than Munch's moonlit painting,
dark vibrating columns set off
by the white throat above the white dress?

Though we run before we walk, and dance
before we sing, that soon the voice
wanders into your walking, and the wind
flies over in packets like an owl of air.

At the top you are a spur
on the backbone of the mountain,
divide the beating city
from the random moor.
Everything's alive, don't worry.

The Shop for Forgotten Things

conveniently, is on your way home,
in fact, on your very block.
It's small, but big enough to hold
all the forgotten things. The fresh dill
you meant to get for your fish,
cream for coffee, new batteries.
The keeper knows all your needs,
anticipates your mnemonic gaps.
To judge from the stock, your neighbors
forget all the same things.
Climb onto the shelf.
Live in hope.

Twilight's Over

Twilight's over but night won't fall.
Clouds with orange pedestals hold up the dark.
It's cool for summer. Women cross their arms
and walk that way, unless they're drunk.
The general condition is somewhere between
depression and death, much giggling
disguises this. You can be invisible
in this light, is that what you want?
Careful study of where people are going
shows they don't know where to go.
And you, my stranger, don't you dread
your strangeness, don't you weep for it?

In the Parking Lot near the Cultural Center

I stood for an hour behind a parked red van,
against a wall of flat stones that smelled
of piss from Friday night's drunks.
I was noticed by parents arriving with their kids
and by people I didn't see, in apartments.
Through the windshield and a side panel
I could see my life: my woman, her sister,
her child with my child's name,
some friends we had fifteen years ago.
And my replacement, for whose obvious pleasure
I know every reason. None of them
thinks of me except when I'm in the paper,
where I try to be as often as I can
so as to intrude without the nastiness
of having to see them. I suppose a dream
disturbs her now and then. It's not
for lack of nerve I didn't stroll
through the parking lot and plunk down
in their smooth Saturday afternoon,
but because they would have talked to me as if they could see me,
and looking straight through them I would have grown tired,
felt nothing. So I watched
their normal life and spared us all
disturbance. *Mama,
who was that man?*

III
Whisper Dance

Who Are the Poets?

Who are the poets to tell you about sex?
Aren't they a population like the rest,
hedonist or prudish, wise, repressed,
dreamy realistic blasé or obsessed,
romantic cynical relaxed or stressed,
experienced innocent cursed and blessed
by Mom and Dad and luck or loneliness?
Better them than shrinks, I guess,
but best
to delve in.

You Don't Have to Be Leonard Cohen

You don't have to be Leonard Cohen to screw
eighteen-year-old girls, you just
have to be eighteen.
Otherwise you'll have to take the hard
road and get famous.

Memento Amori

Heat and humidity give the air an unexpected message.
You're almost naked and your sweat
evaporates in the slight breeze.
The air touches your skin. It's not much
of a touch, just enough
to remind you.

Bananas

The forecast is bananas. Tomorrow:
partly bananas with a chance
of grape showers. I got it bad
and that ain't good. Time
on my hands. Ain't misbehavin',
nothin' happens to me, no no
you can't take that away from me—
nothing minus nothing is the same
as before. I remember April.
I remember a thirtyish woman
waiting on a movie line
with a gray-haired man in Manhattan
in the 20th century, her thin dress clung
to her large hemispherical breasts
and revealed the raised dots of her areolae,
not to mention her long, relaxed nipples.
I also remember the number
of my post office box.

Friday Night

It's Friday night and my balls are enormous,
they don't know it's the Sabbath and they ought to take a rest.
Glands have no religion,
in them there is no east or west,
or day or night, or anything
but response to stimuli or lack thereof.
All the rest is cooked up
by the brain of the beholder,
eye of the loner,
memories growing colder,
counter-current cooling,
spermatic chords.

My Head

My head's more private than my genitals,
it won't go along now and then
with reciprocal exploitation.

Wrong Directions

I was given the wrong directions.
They said the white frame house
but at the top of the hill
there was only a lagoon.
They said Entrance W
but it should have been R,
which I missed and wound up in Out.
On the city grid the numbers were plain
but mine was missing,
and in the country there were never left and right,
just curves and embankments.
Every mountain had a cairn: people
had been there, no question, I found
a snapshot along with the beer bottles:
men sucking pacifiers
and women wearing mother-of-pearl earrings.
On the back I read
"Go straight ahead
till you come to the green sign."
A child's handwriting
that I didn't believe for a minute.

Side Trips

When I've left my house behind
and rented a place in another city
only to travel from there and live
in a hotel overlooking a harbor,
the mountains across the water
remind me of Everest and the series of base camps
the climbers extend to approach the summit,
each in thinner air than the last.
Though I know I'm moving crablike not upward
and may well arrive nowhere but a patch
of wet sand that's home to insects,
the alternating choking and euphoria
save the analogy, don't you think?

But then, my house too is only an outpost
in a city I did not come from,
and the city I came from was not where I was born,
my parents came from there but had moved away,
and their parents had crossed two oceans in opposite directions
and never went back.
Nothing but outposts all the way,
encampments in time and air
that are tenuous by now;
nothing but side trips from sideways trips,
and in the dusk a close-up view
of an oddly familiar claw.

Past

Past midnight past the middle and so what if
the piano is lyrical, the bass is singing and the drums
caress these sounds. Put your hand
over your eyes. Is there a certain
smell? You can't find it but still believe
past testimony. Only,
it's past the past now.

In the movies jazz is a backdrop
for figures who float into clubs,
their lives float too or
drive or drift but always
in a direction, there's a future just offscreen,
the woman trusts the man and he deserves it.

Past the middle of the forest you wander
into town, the hotel, through the bar,
past the corner, into the center
where the bassist stands between piano and drums
and the talkers at the back keep dinning the space
between the piano's lyrical notes,
and the ones who came to listen shake their heads.
In the space between the notes a certain smell
around your eyes that someone found once, but
it wasn't enough, why should
the smallest thing be? Well, because
these are the silent emblems, the spaces
that make notes melody
so time will stop for a few hours
for anyone sitting alone here.

Past time is where you want to be
when trying to be in it gets too long, too steadily

deafening, drilling, dizzying.
This is not the movies. Nothing resolves.
Oh bassist, draw your bow.

Questions

If your life keeps flashing before you,
does that mean you're dying?
If your life stops flashing before you,
does that mean you're dead
or occupied with living—
or could it mean one or the other,
depending? If sunshine and smoke
both make you sneeze, are you healthy
and is there any connection outside you
between sunshine and smoke?
Can you guess a woman's reading habits
from her tattoos? Or from her constant
twisted chewing of her own mucosa?
What accounts for the 70-year decline
in the wardrobe of poets, or the use of gravel
on the ground where music is played outdoors?
Why do people attend to details first
and the big things later or not at all?
Why do they think one thing compensates for another,
though they feel no consolation?
If you find beauty depressing, is your life
worth living? If your life is worth living,
will you find beauty uplifting or neutral?
Why are people, the talking species,
most afraid of talking to other people?
When will eye contact replace fear, and when
will contact replace the tyranny of the eye?
Will the USA ever grow up about sex?
Will suntans ever go out of fashion?
Will ad agencies ever be tried for crimes against humanity?
Will fulfilment ever show its face
to a person who asks questions?

Baul

When the singer begins.
When the singer has begun to drum and begins,
when his foot with its cluster of bells has joined the drum and he begins
    to sing,
the faces of the people seated on floor and bench and chair
are all smiles, their bare and socked feet are smiling too—
private concert, singer all the way
from Bangladesh—but when he has sung a while
of how the soul cannot be kept within the body—
impossible, he says, impossible to do that but also to translate
what the song says is impossible—when his dark voice
has risen in plaited complaint and the ornaments too
have carried upward their own quavering cries,
the corners of mouths turn down, the gazes wander inward,
each person finds a private translation.

As the singer continues, the bells and drums get older,
they go back a thousand years, the voice
gets older, for millennia it has traveled,
has collected many turns and left behind its own,
the wailing tremolo of Hebrew prayers, the smoky chant
of Nubian oud-players. "The man of the heart—
where is he? The woman of the heart—where is she?
Who is she?" Or "If God will not come to you,
you must come to God," the gaze turning inward,
the thought unbidden: Easier to find God
than the woman of the heart, or the man.

Reunion

We went into the earth, under
the reservoir. From a box near the door
I chose a black skullcap, the cave
opened, a crowd of schoolboys
sat in tiers, frozen gestures, pasty
skin. We filled the side galleries.
For eight hours we prayed. And a few of them
moved, the nod of a head, or an arm
abducted one inch. Then nothing.
Like depleted cells after a rest
they'd yielded a final twitch
and were dead: Had we revived them
or killed them? Would they rot now?
We would wait and see.
Until older selves came to pray.

In the Small of the Night

In the small of the night you recall
when there were special days
that came around reliably, naively
confident that your store
of celebration would be large enough
for their needs. They've careened
out of orbit one by one—
birthdays and newyears fall
across colder planes,
Passovers wander off in the sands,
and the miracle of lights is an affair
for other people's children.
Only the Day of Atonement retains
its genius, knowing you cannot exhaust
your supply of regrets. That is why
you hate it—and must atone
for that.

Art Institute

Even the sun for the first time
on the towers of Chicago (like
New York when it still worked)
is not what you wanted, you left
all this to find another sort of room
and on the broad sidewalks the words
of your other language spring from your mouth
in a cry of double loss.
Your past and your future
a bird and its shadow
joined at the feet in the cup
of a Plains Indian bowl,
and to one side a hole the years
have run out through.

And yet. Look. Here in the glass case
one shard of decorated vessel
protrudes at eye level, bearing one eye
of a face long gone, it is peering at you
like your own isolated eye
pressed against the window
in Karl's portrait. The glass stops
the bridge of nose, and the one-eyed gawker
surveys in flat vision the three-dimensional world
he cannot reach.

That Time of the Night (CBC Radio)

At 6 a.m. you have no friends, not even
in another time zone.
You have a flashlight and a radio and an Icelandic sweater
with holes at the elbows
which will keep you alive until the sun
rises theoretically behind rainclouds, in a city
where you live but don't belong, behind
the equally misplaced onion domes.

You've been asleep again, but where is that?
It's one thing to dwell so hard
you take your logy mental goods along
as the angle dips and you slide
into something that feels like thinking
on another plane. Down
in that grave space the planetary voices
exchange their earnest fields of force
until the dance exhausts them and they subside
into their latent clay.
But to drift without will
to another zone, that country
where you belong and have rested your head
on hip and belly in the lawny night,
to be back in that life
of skin and scent and the easy match of nested overláp—
until it happens and her return to these quilts
is from a private phone call you've waited through
with your feet at the pillow and your blood
suddenly without a line
so you fall

and are wide awake on a bed of dull
questions that have torqued you before.

Elsewhere, as you run in vain
through names in the already woken half of the world,
people you know are alive in rooms
where breezes swell the colored curtains
and a glance acknowledges each hum
as the scents of the garden enter;
and others are engaged in their tasks or have long since unpacked
survival kits they consider picnics
and don't want to be reminded.
Here you can only circle the carpet
and hear its slight synthetic brush
against your synthetic sock,
and hear the replayed voice of a woman
revealing from her post on the prairies
that she needs some mail,
that behind the music said to make one enivré,
she is in a studio,
sober as the short grass.

Whisper Dance

Once you couldn't see the dance yet for the dancers
and in your non-youth at times
it happens again, as tonight L'Esquisse
"fractures silence" with fated speech
darkened by a backdrop of later music,
or with mute dancing but always
the dancers' beauty is crushing, their bodies
like the taped speech from that long-ago
once in your life, before their own birth,
and indeed they pass through doors, they
rush out seeking, meet for a time,
withdraw and close them only to move these doors
and open them again, the women
ride the doors, climb the doors,
stand whispering to the doorposts in every Romance
language, whispers the men who dance before them
can't make out—you can't decipher them either
though you can hear the *s*'s and Italian *c*'s,
can hear the dancers breathing when they
stop, lie still.
         Yes the dance
takes you in at intervals, but still the bodies
call their descending chords in you
until you wonder if they distract each other,
if now a man remembers that he'll never put his hand
just there on just this woman
except in the quasi-chaste movement when she arcs the air
so it bends to the will of virtual forces,
motives beyond us.
                 The women
suffer themselves to be leapt
and suffer themselves to be caught,

when they are tired they close the doors
and the men must find other occupations.

Who are they, this troupe whose names alone
the program gives; and who could crack
the silence of these etymologies? Their names
are doors I can't pass through,
thresholds they have barely learned to stand on.
Paraklausithyron.
The dance through the dancers
I take away, dance to doors
that whisper back: On the other side,
no, the *other* side, you will find,
yes certo seguro bien sur, all you need
is to open, open, and open again.

Notes

The poems were written over an extended period and are not presented in chronological order.

In the Crowd
    "matches": in case a smoker should need a light

The Human Genome
    "trykkfeil": Norwegian for typographical errors.

Why I Am Not an Indian
    I have been asked by more than one person in Norway whether I am an Indian. For a decade or two, when some Scandinavian writers with at least one Jewish grandparent found it appealing to declare they were Jewish, they were often met with the question, "What percentage?" This was a neutral request for information.

Twilight's Over
    With thanks to Dennis Schmitz for his book title, *We Weep for Our Strangeness*.

Bananas
    With nods for songs, as follows:
    "I Got It Bad and That Ain't Good": Duke Ellington and Paul Francis Webster
    "Time on My Hands": Vincent Youmans, Harold Adamson, and Mack Gordon
    "Ain't Misbehavin'": Fats Waller, Harry Brooks, and Andy Razaf
    "Everything Happens to Me": Tom Adair and Matt Dennis
    "They Can't Take That Away from Me": George and Ira Gershwin
    "I'll Remember April": Gene de Paul, Patricia Johnston, and Don Raye

Friday Night
    "chords" is an intentional spelling.

Baul
    A Baul is a mystic singer from Bengal.

That Time of the Night
    The title of a classical music program on CBC FM. The program host when I wrote this poem was Katherine Duncan.

Acknowledgments

"Why I Am Not an Indian" was published in a slightly different form in the anthology *101 Jewish Poems for the Third Millennium*.

Thanks to the journals in which the following poems first appeared:
"Reunion": *Pequod*
"Rollback": *Saturday Night*
"The Voice," "Twilight's Over," "Biology," "Wrong Directions": *ARS-INTERPRES: An International Annual of Poetry, Translation & Art*
"Spring Flowers at Pompeii": *ELQ (Exile Magazine)*
"Office Workers Looking at the Sky": *Stand Magazine*
"Welcome Back / Come Again": *The Manhattan Review*
"In the Crowd": *Poetry East*

My thanks to those who have read drafts of the manuscript of this book or parts of it and have offered me comments and suggestions: Richard M. Lush, Richard Strier, Peter Anson, Jay Parini, Kevin Prufer, and Robert David Cohen.

BLACK WIDOW PRESS

POETRY IN TRANSLATION

Approximate Man and Other Writings by Tristan Tzara. Translated and edited by Mary Ann Caws.

Art Poétique by Guillevic. Translated by Maureen Smith.

Beginnings of the Prose Poem. Edited by Mary Ann Caws, Michel Delville.

The Big Game by Benjamin Péret. Translated with an introduction by Marilyn Kallet.

Boris Vian Invents Boris Vian: A Boris Vian Reader. Edited and translated by Julia Older.

Capital of Pain by Paul Eluard. Translated by Mary Ann Caws, Patricia Terry, and Nancy Kline.

Chanson Dada: Selected Poems by Tristan Tzara. Translated with an introduction and essay by Lee Harwood.

Earthlight (Clair de Terre) by André Breton. Translated by Bill Zavatsky and Zack Rogow. (New and revised edition.)

Essential Poems and Prose of Jules Laforgue. Translated and edited by Patricia Terry.

Essential Poems and Writings of Joyce Mansour: A Bilingual Anthology. Translated with an introduction by Serge Gavronsky.

Essential Poems and Writings of Robert Desnos: A Bilingual Anthology. Edited with an introduction and essay by Mary Ann Caws.

EyeSeas (Les Ziaux) by Raymond Queneau. Translated with an introduction by Daniela Hurezanu and Stephen Kessler.

Fables in a Modern Key by Pierre Coran. Translated by Norman R. Shapiro. Full-color illustrations by Olga Pastuchiv.

Fables of Town & Country by Pierre Coran. Translated by Norman R. Shapiro. Full-color illustrations by Olga Pastuchiv.

A Flea the Size of Paris: The Old French Fatrasies & Fatras. Edited and translated by Ted Byrne and Donato Mancini.

Forbidden Pleasures: New Selected Poems 1924–1949 by Luis Cernuda. Translated by Stephen Kessler.

Furor and Mystery & Other Writings by René Char. Translated by Mary Ann Caws and Nancy Kline.

The Gentle Genius of Cécile Périn: Selected Poems (1906–1956). Edited and translated by Norman R. Shapiro.

The Great Madness by Avigdor Hameiri. Translated and edited by Peter C. Appelbaum with an introduction by Dan Hecht.

Guarding the Air: Selected Poems of Gunnar Harding. Translated and edited by Roger Greenwald.

Howls & Growls: French Poems to Bark By. Translated by Norman R. Shapiro; illustrated by Olga K. Pastuchiv.

I Have Invented Nothing: Selected Poems by Jean-Pierre Rosnay. Translated by J. Kates.

In Praise of Sleep: Selected Poems of Lucian Blaga. Translated with an introduction by Andrei Codrescu

The Inventor of Love & Other Writings by Gherasim Luca. Translated by Julian & Laura Semilian. Introduction by Andrei Codrescu. Essay by Petre Răileanu.

Jules Supervielle: Selected Prose and Poetry. Translated by Nancy Kline & Patricia Terry.

La Fontaine's Bawdy by Jean de La Fontaine. Translated with an introduction by Norman R. Shapiro.

Last Love Poems of Paul Eluard.
Translated with an introduction by Marilyn Kallet.

A Life of Poems, Poems of a Life by Anna de Noailles.
Edited and translated by Norman R. Shapiro.
Introduction by Catherine Perry.

Love, Poetry (L'amour la poésie) by Paul Eluard.
Translated with an essay by Stuart Kendall.

Of Human Carnage—Odessa 1918–1920 by
Avigdor Hameiri. Translated and edited by Peter
C. Appelbaum with an introduction by Dan
Hecht.

Pierre Reverdy: Poems, Early to Late.
Translated by Mary Ann Caws and Patricia Terry.

Poems of André Breton: A Bilingual Anthology.
Translated with essays by Jean-Pierre Cauvin and
Mary Ann Caws.

Poems of A.O. Barnabooth by Valery Larbaud.
Translated by Ron Padgett and Bill Zavatsky.

Poems of Consummation by Vicente Aleixandre.
Translated by Stephen Kessler.

Préversities: A Jacques Prévert Sampler.
Translated and edited by Norman R. Shapiro.

RhymAmusings (AmuseRimes) by Pierre Coran.
Translated by Norman R. Shapiro.

The Sea and Other Poems by Guillevic. Translated by
Patricia Terry. Introduction by Monique Chefdor.

Sixty Years: Selected Poems 1957–2017
by Mikhail Yeryomin. Translated by J. Kates.

Through Naked Branches by Tarjei Vesaas.
Translated, edited, and introduced by Roger
Greenwald.

To Speak, to Tell You? Poems by Sabine Sicaud.
Translated by Norman R. Shapiro. Introduction
and notes by Odile Ayral-Clause.

MODERN POETRY SERIES

RALPH ADAMO
All the Good Hiding Places: Poems

WILLIS BARNSTONE
ABC of Translation
African Bestiary (forthcoming)

DAVE BRINKS
The Caveat Onus
The Secret Brain: Selected Poems 1995–2012

RUXANDRA CESEREANU
California (on the Someș). Translated by Adam J.
Sorkin
    and Ruxandra Cesereanu.
Crusader-Woman. Translated by Adam J. Sorkin.
    Introduction by Andrei Codrescu.
Forgiven Submarine by Ruxandra Cesereanu
    and Andrei Codrescu.

ANDREI CODRESCU
Forgiven Submarine by Ruxandra Cesereanu
    and Andrei Codrescu.
Too Late for Nightmares: Poems

CLAYTON ESHLEMAN
An Alchemist with One Eye on Fire
Anticline
Archaic Design
Clayton Eshleman/The Essential Poetry: 1960–2015
Grindstone of Rapport: A Clayton Eshleman Reader
Penetralia
Pollen Aria
The Price of Experience
Endure: Poems by Bei Dao. Translated by Clayton
    Eshleman and Lucas Klein.
Curdled Skulls: Poems of Bernard Bador.
    Translated by Bernard Bador with Clayton
    Eshleman.

ROGER GREENWALD
An Opening in the Vertical World
Keener Sounds: A Suite (forthcoming)

PIERRE JORIS
Barzakh (Poems 2000–2012)
Exile Is My Trade: A Habib Tengour Reader

MARILYN KALLET
Even When We Sleep
How Our Bodies Learned
Packing Light: New and Selected Poems
The Love That Moves Me
Disenchanted City (La ville désenchantée)
  by Chantal Bizzini. Translated by J. Bradford Anderson, Darren Jackson, and Marilyn Kallet.

ROBERT KELLY
Fire Exit
The Hexagon

STEPHEN KESSLER
Garage Elegies
Last Call

BILL LAVENDER
Memory Wing

HELLER LEVINSON
from stone this running
jus' sayn'
LinguaQuake
Lure
Lurk
Query Caboodle
Seep
Shift Gristle
Tenebraed
Un-
Valvular Ash
Wrack Lariat

JOHN OLSON
Backscatter: New and Selected Poems
Dada Budapest
Larynx Galaxy
Weave of the Dream King

NIYI OSUNDARE
City Without People: The Katrina Poems
Green: Sighs of Our Ailing Planet: Poems

MEBANE ROBERTSON
An American Unconscious
Signal from Draco: New and Selected Poems

JEROME ROTHENBERG
Concealments and Caprichos
Eye of Witness: A Jerome Rothenberg Reader.
  Edited with commentaries by Heriberto Yepez & Jerome Rothenberg.
The President of Desolation & Other Poems

AMINA SAÏD
The Present Tense of the World: Poems 2000–2009.
Translated with an introduction by Marilyn Hacker.

JULIAN SEMILIAN
Osiris with a trombone across the seam of insubstance

ANIS SHIVANI
Soraya (Sonnets)

JERRY W. WARD, JR.
Fractal Song

ANTHOLOGIES / BIOGRAPHIES

Barbaric Vast & Wild: A Gathering of Outside and Subterranean Poetry (Poems for the Millennium, vol. 5). Jerome Rothenberg and John Bloomberg-Rissman, eds.

Clayton Eshleman: The Whole Art
by Stuart Kendall

Revolution of the Mind: The Life of André Breton
by Mark Polizzotti